T0266568

THE NAOMI POEMS, BOOK ONE:
CORPSE AND BEANS

SAINT GERAUD (1940–1966)

Black Ocean
Boston · Chicago

To reprint, reproduce, or transmit electronically, or by recording all or part of this manuscript, beyond brief reviews or educational purposes, please send a written request to the publisher at:

Black Ocean
P.O. Box 52030
Boston, MA 02205
blackocean.org

Grateful acknowledgement is made to the Estate of Bill Knott for permission to publish these poems.

Cover by Julian Montague | montagueprojects.com
Book design by Janaka Stucky | janakastucky.com

ISBN: 978-1-939568-74-8
LCCN: 2023938560

SECOND EDITION

1 2 3 4 5 6 7 8 9 10

Printed in China using FSC® Certified materials

MIX
Paper | Supporting responsible forestry
FSC® C153458

Acknowledgements and
any credit are due to:

with love and thanks to
Barbara Harr,
who helped and helped

and to
Marjorie Hunt,
who is the best poet I know;
Bill Hunt;
Frances Illgen,
who is so clear, so russet,
that other women
use her shadow
for a mirror;
Robert Bly and family;
Louis Hammer;
Gene Fowler;
William Terry;
and Richard Deutch

and to
Martha Friedberg
who is the most beautiful

CONTENTS

FOREWORD

I would like to write a foreword like a catastrophically messy studio apartment, a hamster nest of Bill Knott. A rainstorm in it too, deluge of Knott obliterating the one-room slum interior. There are pictures of him in such a domicile, though the rain is not there, but rather here in my room, forming sympathetically, streaks of his attacks on my presumption, it is, with tumbling cardboard boxes, books, and whipped plastic bags bombarding and wetly whipping me in anger for saying any of this. Though I have faith, also, that he would forgive me.

I don't want to dwell on his personal life, but it's hard to separate from his work, given that the writing is pervaded by his sense of being unloved and lonely, null. There's no way to disregard how he originally presented himself: as a nobody, not only orphaned but, at 26, dead, as he wished to be described for the original publication of this book, attributed by him fiercely to "St. Geraud (1940–1966)," a name borrowed from the main character of an obscure, centuries-old French pornographic novel in which Geraud presides over a sex-riddled orphanage—fiercely, if also half-heartedly: he did allow it to be stated in the book that it was the work of the living Bill Knott, though nevertheless remaining identified as "a virgin and a suicide."

This was the book and its context that I found sometime within a year of its original publication in 1968 when I was 18 or 19. The package was transporting, like an infection or injection, an all-pervading condition of longing, adoration, fear, and fury, lurching from near-worship of "Naomi" into anger and despair at, among much else, the bloodthirsty American military and their corporate cohort, all in a language of starfish and "barnlight" and "From heart to heart / a heartbeat staggers, looking for a haven." It had a huge impact on me, and I still love Bill Knott (1940–2014) no matter how much he would reject any profession of affection or admiration from anyone.

He was born in a tiny town in farmland Michigan. His father was a butcher, and his mother died in childbirth when the poet was seven (the child, who would have been Knott's only sibling, died too), whereupon his father (who killed himself three years later) sent him to live in an orphanage near Chicago. He was held there until the institution tired of him too, and, at age 15, he was committed to a nearby mental asylum. A year later he was taken in by an uncle to work chores on a failing farm back in Michigan. Upon high school graduation, he spent two years in the army at Fort Knox, KY, followed by nearly a decade as a hospital orderly in Chicago, during which he wrote the poems in this book. Halfway through the bedpan-jockey era, he had a colleague mail out a mimeo'd page to the literary world announcing that he'd committed suicide, primarily because no one loved him.

Knott is in the lineage of Rimbaud and van Gogh and Sylvia Plath for the dramatic resonance of their lives' stories, while also having in common with them that all the anecdotal abjection-glamour is atomized by the power of the works themselves. But he was a human being, and he arrived at his poetry, his methods, in part by routes that can be mapped.

However it may seem inconsistent with his original self-presentation, Knott was markedly factual—forthcoming and forthright—in his relatively few interviews. Clearly his integrity demanded that when asked about his personal and poetic history he do his best to describe it without self-serving distortion (though he did supply two different explanations for his brief adoption of the pen name [1]).

It's reductive to the point of demeaning to refer to Knott as a Surrealist, but he got a lot from André Breton's ideas and that movement's ardent and defiant first practitioners. The

---

[1] "Paranoid fear: I got out of the Army in 1960, and I was supposed to report for reserve duty, but I didn't report, so I thought that the FBI was after me. I thought if I published with my real name someone would see it in my hometown and report me to the draft board. [. . .] I used to have tottering nightmares about having to go through boot camp again—so, I had to use some other name." Interview by Harry Greenberg, *Some* 4, Summer 1973.

"[T]he answer is: Pretentiousness. Stupidity. I justified it to myself at the time by noting that two of my then-favorites (Eluard and Neruda, neither of whom mean much to me now) were pen-named poets. I wanted to emulate them." Interview by Adam Travis at *Bookslut* website, 2005, as preserved at www.billknottarchive.com/interviews.

conception of Surrealism now, a century after Breton, tends to be cartoony and superficial, but the original poets were uncompromising seers and activists, and their more recent descendants have remained unconventional and inspired. Latter-day American poets who benefitted greatly from Surrealism include John Ashbery and, inadvertently/chimerically, James Tate—a collaborator and sometime idol of Knott's—as well as Knott himself. Also central to Knott's development were the sensibility and views of Robert Bly and the poets affirmed by him in his magazines *The Fifties* and *The Sixties*, and possibly even *The Seventies*, in which Bly pointed American writers towards the richness of whole cosmoses of poetry little known here because they weren't written in English, such as Gottfried Benn, Juan Ramón Jimenez, César Vallejo, Blas de Otero, Federico García Lorca, and Tomas Tranströmer, most of whom were either influenced by Surrealism or had values in common with it. Bly advocated for "leaping poetry," a concept related to Surrealism in its insistence on the importance of the writers' receptivity to, reliance on, the unconscious.

Knott repeatedly emphasized in interviews how important it was to him to have had the benefit of searching out translations, often citing a Kenneth Rexroth essay on the subject as his original prompt: "The point of his essay was, as I understood it then and now, that since young poets inevitably have to imitate their predecessors, they would be better off imitating foreign poets. If you imitated Creeley (as I had done for a period, so Rexroth's example struck home to me), you took on his style, his language, as well as his content. But with Leopardi, you could only copy his content. You couldn't adopt his voice and stylistic rhythms, you would be forced to concoct your own. This made so much sense to me at the time that I quickly began reading more poets in translation, consciously seeking my models in them."[2]

Knott's original and most significant formal teacher was John Logan, whose poem about Rimbaud, "Lives of the Poet," Knott had discovered in the mass-market anthology/periodical *New World Writing* when he was still in a rural Michigan high school (ca. 1957), thereby inspired to make his first stabs at writing poems. After leaving the Army, when he relocated to Chicago (1960), he found that Logan was teaching an adult-education poetry workshop at the University of Chicago, and he enrolled. Thereafter, for a few years, Logan's poetry itself as well as his poetic values would be major influences on Knott's writing. Logan was also in the network of American poets that Bly admired and published in his magazine, and it was via Logan that Knott also met Paul Carroll, who would be the editor and publisher, with Big Table / Follett, of the original *Naomi Poems*.

Another interesting thing to learn from Knott's interviews is that his poems tended to be collages, or compilations. While his colleague Tate's procedure was to "go on nerve,"

---

[2] Interview by Robert Arnold, *Memorious* 6, June 2006 [and www.billknottarchive.com/interviews].

Frank O'Hara– / Bette Davis–style, and surprise himself with line after line into the unknown, Knott kept notebooks full of individual lines and concepts, saved for their wild beauty and evocative power, not to mention humor, though not otherwise associated with Knott's personal life per se, "Because I don't write out of personal experience, I keep notebooks and I have lines and images and I keep searching for where I can put them in. So it seems I can never start a poem and know what it's going to be about before I finish it, know what's going to be in it. [. . .] I've probably got 100 [notebooks] by now. I have lost some of them over the years. I mine them when I'm putting a poem together. So the finished poem is an amalgam of varying moods and even language."[3] (I would suppose "Eternity," on p. 2, is a prime example of this.) Also: "I think my attention span is about two seconds cuz I can't write about anything for more than two lines. The great failure of my poems is that every second line I change the subject, or write on lots of stuff and then try to cram it altogether into one thing, and it doesn't work."[4]

An edifying illustration of the complexity of Knott's branching and interwoven techniques and aims and motivations could be to consider the subtitle of this book: Corpse and Beans. *The Naomi Poems: Corpse and Beans.*

---

[3] Interview by James Randall, *Ploughshares* Vol. 4, No. 1, 1977, p.13 [and www.billknottarchive.com/interviews].

[4] Interview by Harry Greenberg, *Some* 4, Summer 1973, p. 33.

What the hell is that about? The words "The Naomi Poems"
sound tender, if dark—romantic; minor-key musical . . .

> And Naomi was sown. She crossed the boundaries
> of wounds to kneel in the snowfall at the center.
> Her palms upon my forehead became my fever's petals.
> Her face—Arc de Triomphe of sadness, altar where my
>   heart is solved—
> created for me its absence in the ark of its cheekbones.

—from "Last Poem"

Why'd he have to corpse and bean it? Because he wants the
full-bodied reality. :-) In the mid-sixties, one of the most
important writers for Knott was the original Surrealist poet
Robert Desnos (born 1900, died in a concentration camp
1945), and one of Desnos's books was *Corps et biens*, which
translates as "bodies and goods" or "crew and cargo"—a
phrase associated with its use in the context of olden-days
shipwrecks, when all aboard, along with the freight, are lost
at sea. "Corpse and beans" is a homophonic translation
of "corps et biens." But it doesn't stop there. The full-
scale book of poems that Knott published subsequent to
Naomi was called *Auto-Necrophilia* (!), and it includes the
following poem:

CORPSE AND BEANS, OR
WHAT IS POETRY?

I sit at my table and sometimes the question of poetry
    crosses my mind
For example
        The man who one night ate a big plate
    of beans
Then got tired
        Of everything and killed himself
Next day at the burial
Everyone said, What's that noise?

Was it poetry?

The poet wonders, in love.[5]

—Richard Hell
New York, 2024

---

[5] He died at 74 on the operating table where he was getting heart surgery in 2014. He'd earned his living as a poetry professor at Emerson College in Boston for most of the latter half of his life. Though widely and steadily published, he continued to bitterly complain of being a despised failure. After 2000 he put all his hundreds and hundreds of poems online where they can still be found at the posthumous billknottarchive.com, which site also preserves four of the five interviews I'm aware of and have used for the biographical information here (further fact-checked elsewhere). The fifth interview, a fantastic 14 pages' worth, is to be found in the small NYC literary magazine *Some* 4, Summer 1973.

THE NAOMI POEMS, BOOK ONE:
CORPSE AND BEANS

POEM

Alright if I have to be famous let it be for this great
    starfish-shield I made
And the sands of her face drift over her body

ETERNITY

I stick my head into a womb and make faces at the unborn
I walk down my dead ends to the beach
Fossils from the future, tongs to nip the eye
Your etude profile
A crater is the total opera
Alberto Giacometti master-criminal
We had just fallen off
Of a scream
O boat of black mane
Sail heals the leper waves at a touch
A kiss restores wombsight to our limbs
It has been found
What
It has not been found
The waves nail upon the sand your escape
To where starfish are pointing

POEM

Night, in whose death did your ennui take refuge?
The women all lay their kerchiefs on the water, and stepped
    back

KAREZZAS, CUNTRAS, COCKTURNES,
MANSHRIEKS, CARRIONCRIES

the holy tides are being written
by the young of all times and lights poets
dancing psychedelicately
playing, saying "One
    in my hand, one in the air, and one in you"

        —for the Human Be-ins and young rock poets
        jugglers heads

VOI (POEM) CES

"mercy . . . mercy" From face to face
a child's voice bounces, lower and lower;
continues its quest
underground.

Bloodspurts lessening . . . hoofbeats of animals
stalked to their birth by the sun, fade. It is a bright
edgeless morning, like a knife that to be cleaned
is held under a vein.

I blink away the stinging gleam
as my country sows desert upon Vietnam.
We, imperious, die of human thirst
—having forgotten tears are an oasis.

"help . . . help" From heart to heart
a heartbeat staggers, looking for a haven.
Bereft. It is easier to enter heaven
than to pass through each others' eyes,

pores,
armor,
like merciful sperm, cool water, the knife—
thrust of tears. . . . It is easier
to go smoothly insane—like a Detroit car—
than to stammer and hiccup help.

And this poem is the easiest thing of all:
it floats upon children's singing, out of the bloodstream;
a sunbeam shoulders it, carries it away.
There is nothing left.

                "yes . . . yes there is"

RETORT TO PASTERNAK

The centuries like barges have floated
out of the darkness, to communism: not to be judged,
but to be unloaded.

POEM
for Marion Helz

When our hands are alone,
they open, like faces.
There is no shore
to their opening.

THREE STANZAS FOR YVETTE MIMIEUX

Your shadow leaps down from the sun to
Hold its happy half your cheek swells towards
The unsheared blood of summer ting
Ling morning awake your kisses play at sleep

Apronlapful of green ripples picked
From their first kiss fragrant voice
Crowned slumberess of days your
Body is a dance that rhymes the four

Winds

I only keep this voice to give to anything afraid of me

SUMMER

an afternoon walk
your hair the color of barnlight
there's the field this is the river
our first loving has reached the sea by now
(where it'll meet and embrace our childhood)
we bathe in the flow of a mute woman's happiness
sitting on the bank dangling and drifting on the water
come back
the flowers nuzzle our joined hands

LOVE—A POEM

I lay in her humus breaths
And she was fulfilling her essence
As music perfume wine of future loves
Whose birth she was lighting in me

Nakedness exists only an instant
Quickly becomes flesh, becomes thought
Nakedness flares to light up love
To resurrect the present with a touch

The night is a torch of comas
Wondering, I look at lovers
Each inhales the other's visions
And they burn deeply, like a torch of comas

*

To read the future, gaze into your crystal asshole

POEM

Let the dead bury the dead:
it is said. But I say it is we living
who have been shoved underground, who must now rise up
to bury the dead, the Johnsons, Francos, Fords and
      McNamaras.

SONG

Naomi looks for her child
in the trees, in the leaves.
It is of fire, and has spirited her away.
Though sea-level rise to heart-level,
in the trees, in the leaves.

POEM

The beach holds and sifts us through her dreaming fingers
Summer fragrances green between your legs
At night, naked auras cool the waves
Vanished
O Naomi
I kiss every body of you, every face

POEM

What language will be safe
When we lie awake all night
Saying palm words, no fingertip words
This wound searching us for a voice
Will become a fountain with rooms to let
Or a language composed of kisses and leaves

POEM

My eyelids close on your nipples, enclosing them.
When we wake—

POEM

Far final peaks, burn off this sleep,
use it as fuel in your endless creation of the pure face!

GOODBYE

If you are still alive when you read this,
close your eyes. I am
under their lids, growing black.

NOTE

I left a
right where the nipple cheeps
kiss in each nest
of the black bra
hung inside your bathroom door

TO AMERICAN POETS

I

There's no time left to write poems.
If you will write rallyingcries, yes, do so,
otherwise write poems then throw yourselves on the river
  to drift away.
Li Po's peach-blossom, even if it departs this world, can't
  help us.
Pound's or Williams' theories on prosody don't meet the
  cries of dying children
(whose death I think is no caesura).
Soon there will be no ideas but in things,
in rubble, in skulls held under the oceans' magnifying-glass,
in screams driven into one lightning-void.
Only you can resurrect the present. People
need your voice to come among them like nakedness,
to fuse them into one marching language in which the word
  "peace" will be said for the last time.
Write slogans, write bread that pounds the table for silence,
write what I can't imagine: words to wake me and all those
who slump over like sapped tombstones when the generals
  talk.
The world is not divided into your schools of poetry.
No: there are the destroyers—the Johnsons, Kys, Rusks,
  Hitlers, Francos—then there are those
they want to destroy—lovers, teachers, plows, potatoes:

this is the division. You
are not important. Your black mountains, solitary farms,
LSD trains. Don't forget: you are important.
If you fail, there will be no-one left to say so.
If you succeed, there will also be a great silence. Your names,
     an open
secret in all hearts, no-one will say. But everywhere
they will be finishing the poems you broke away from.

2

What I mean is: maybe you are the earth's last poets.
Li Po's riverbank poems are far, far out in eternity—
but a nuclear war could blow us that far in an instant:
there's no time left.
Tolstoy's "I would plow."
Plow, plow. But with no-one left to seed, reap,
you write? O rocks are
shortlived as man now. But still this BillyBuddworld
blesses its murderers with Spring even as I write this . . .
so I have nowhere else to turn to but you.
Old echoes are useless. Glare from
the fireball this planet will become already makes shadows
     of us.
There's Einstein. —The light
of poems streaking through space, growing younger, younger,
becoming the poet again somewhere? No!
What I mean is. . . .

PROSEPOEM

Each evening the sea casts starfish up on the beach, scattering, stranding them. They die at dawn, leaving black hungers in the sun. We slept there that summer, we fucked in their radiant evolutions up to our body. Ringed by starfish gasping for their element, we joined to create ours. All night they inhaled the sweat from our thrusting limbs, and lived. Often she cried out: Your hand! —It was a starfish, caressing her with my low fire.

POEM TO POETRY
for Jennifer Kidney

Poetry,
you are an electric,
a magic, field—like the space
between a sleepwalker's outheld arms . . .

TO WHAT'S-HER-NAME

You have lived your life by
the "scorched earth" policy—destroying
everything before that advancing enemy, death. . . . or love.

As when an earthquake gazes at us, you are still
untouched. Laughing you put the torch to
lovers, poems, overture of dawn upon the fields,
your beautiful Ann-Margaret-like thighs scarred by ikons,
legends and waters: your green feelers
—but you are no Bitch Russia!

As you fall back to your least heart,
war will arrive: when I come
upon you cowering behind your last grassblade
I'll laugh and sweep on. Then you will begin
to burn the deserts.

MOZART

Mozart—when you were kissing a woman's cunt, were you never afraid of kissing your own slimy, shrunken pate emerging from within?

FOOTNOTE TO "MOZART"

Why Mozart? The prodigy. He begins his art at a very early age, thus comes close to kissing his birth.

PROSEPOEM

Near the sea the big captain horse found a child's ear-print in the sand. Ah, he said, and put his head faithfully to it. The roughneck sky laughed and pointed and hooted, until the big horse grew very red about the ears and went away. Was she listening?

POEM

I am one man, worshipping silk knees,
picking myself from between my teeth,
I write these lines to cripple the dead,
to come up halt before the living:

I am one man, I run my hand over
your body, I touch the secret vibes
of the earth, I breathe your
heartbeat, Naomi, and always

I am one man alone at night. I fill my hands
with your dark hair
and offer it to the hollows of your face. I am one man,
　　　searching,
alone at night
like a beacon of ashes. . . .

POEM

The only response
to a child's grave is
to lie down before it and play dead

POEM

My sperm is lyre in your blood your
Smell wanders over me like a mouth
You die a moment in my eyes then pass through into my
    heart
Where you live as a drunk
Where you live as that body burnt
Naked by the throes of your whitest name
River carving a deathmask for these words
I paint the features of a face on the head of my cock
But I don't call it Orpheus
Bridge between love and paper between dream and quick-
    sand I
You salt tongued to idea abyss' gaze
Our sunglasses broken like *ciao*
All of time battles your instant
You lie under cool enormous leaves once the sun's eyelids
Your instant—into which dies mine and eternity's and our's
Sweat-bead upon your belly

(POEM) (CHICAGO) (THE WERE-AGE)

"My age, my beast!"—Osip Mandelstam

On the lips a taste of tolling we are blind
The light drifts like dust over faces
We wear masks on our genitals
You've heard of lighting cigarettes with banknotes we used
    to light ours with Jews
History is made of bricks you can't go through it
And bricks are made of bones and blood and
Bones and blood are made of little tiny circles that nothing
    can go through
Except a piano with rabies
Blood gushes into, not from, our wounds
Vietnamese Cuban African bloods
Drunk as dogs before our sons
The bearded foetus lines up at the evolution-trough
Swarmy bloods in the rabid piano
The air over Chicago is death's monogram
This is the Were-Age rushing past
Speed: 10,000 men per minute
This is the species bred of death
The manshriek of flesh
The lifeless sparks of flesh

Covering the deep drums of vision
O new era race-wars jugular-lightning
Dark glance bursting from the over-ripe future
Know we are not the smilelines of dreams
Nor the pores of the Invisible
Piano with rabies we are victorious over
The drum and the wind-chime
We bite back a voice that might have emerged
To tame these dead bodies and wet ashes

(SERGEY) (YESENIN) SPEAKING
(ISADORA) (DUNCAN)

I love Russia; and Isadora in her dance.
When I put my arms around her, she's like
Wheat that sways in the very midst of a bloody battle,
—Unharkened-to, but piling up peace for the earth
(Though my self-war juggles no nimbus) Earthquakes;
    shoulders
A-lit with birthdays of doves; piety of the unwashable
Creases in my mother's gaze and hands. Isadora "becalmed"
Isadora the ray sky one tastes on the skin of justborn babies
(Remember, Isadora
When you took me to America
                              I went, as one visits a grave, to
The place where Bill Knott would be born 20 years in the
    future
I embraced: the pastures, the abandoned quarry, where he
    would play
With the children of your aura and my sapling eye
Where bees brought honey to dying flowers I sprinkled
Childhood upon the horizons, the cows
Who licked my heart like a block of salt) Isadora I write
    this poem
On my shroud, when my home-village walks out to harvest.
Bread weeps as you break it gently into years.

AFTER THE BURIAL

After the burial I alone stood by till 2 workmen came to shovel the dirst back into the hole. There was some left over, the dirt she'd displaced, and they wheeled it off. Drawn, not knowing why, I followed at a distance. Coming to a small backlot, they dumped it, then left. I walked over. It made a small mound. And all around her, similar mounds. Pure cones of joy! First gifts from the dead! I fell to my knees before it, and fell forward on my hands into it . . . to the elbows, like washwater. . . . For the first time, I became empty enough to cry for her.

DEATH

Going to sleep, I cross my hands on my chest.
They will place my hands like this.
It will look as though I am flying into myself.

POEM FOR IRENE KELLER,
WHO ASKED FOR ONE

If all your bones were candles,
your face would still be a dark answer.

If your smells were wind-chimes,
breezes would leave too late to reach their destination,
would arrive at their predestination.

And if your skin were sheets of paper,
my ashes blown over them would make
the lines I meant to not write.

Chimera dressed in chimeras:
if you were this poem
I would not be its writer.

(FARMBOY) (DREAMING) (NIGHTSTORM)

I skiffed up rivers and creeks of lightning
till thunder
split my covers
and down I drowned
lung by lung to a stone
of barnacle-cold salt
the cows licked.

SLEEP

We brush the other, invisible moon.
Its caves come out and carry us inside.

POEM

After your death,
Naomi, your hair will escape to become
a round animal, nameless.

SECRETARY

McNamara the businessman sits at his desk
And stamps "PAID" on the death-lists

Naomi, why did you give parts of you to other women when you left, your hair to that one, your eyes to this, your mouth to another, and why did you command them to follow and haunt me? To keep me in thrall? If you were kind, I would say it was to help me forget you in stages, a little at a time. But never fear: I will always bear the tattoo from your deathcamp.

HAIR POEM

Hair is heaven's water flowing eerily over us
Often a woman drifts off down her long hair and is lost

POEM

At your light side trees shy
A kneeling enters them

NUREMBURG, U.S.A.

In this time and place, where "Bread and Circuses" has
become "Bread and Atrocities," to say 'I love you' is
like saying the latest propaganda phrase . . . 'defoliation' . . .
        'low yield blast'.
If bombing children is preserving peace, then
my fucking you is a war-crime.

LAST POEM

It's harder and harder to whistle you up from my pack of
    dead,
you lag back, loping in another love.
Fate is lucky not to have known you as I have known you.
One dawn the menstrual face of time found, frozen upon
    stones,
pore-song of the poet. Rigor mortis walked the streets, its
coat tattered, face pensive. A howl was heard, calming
    chimeras.

My hair strikes me a great blow.
Wine lifts its deep sky over us.

And Naomi was sown. She crossed the boundaries
of wounds to kneel in the snowfall at the center.
Her palms upon my forehead became my fever's petals.
Her face—Arc de Triomphe of sadness, altar where my heart
    is solved—
created for me its absence in the ark of its cheekbones.

Girls tie their hair together and run as one
woman through my voiceland. Ground-glass sings my
    statues,
those who can only kiss wound-to-wound are born.

Your face alone has no echo in the void. Your face, more
        marvelous
each time it flows up your warm arms to break
upon your smile. Your kisses still rustling in my voice,
you don't exist. I will fill you with
sweet suicide.
Naomi, love other men.
Don't let this be their last poem, only mine.

DEATH

Perfume opens its eyes of you.
I shall be the shepherd of your hair.
A dawn made of all the air I ever breathed.

(NOVEMBER) (LIGHT, SHORT DAYS)
(DARK FIERY SUNSETS)

for Quasimodo

A small bird hops about in branches,
a blue high toss,
the sound
goes. Winter
begins to burn up all the light.

And in no time,
it's evening.
The boy gazes to the west
as if all the fire-engines in the world were streaking there. . . .

POEM TO WOMEN

And I fell through all your absent arms
With the star I had never flung
Desperately back to weld apart my heart

PROSEPOEM

If Hart Crane could have become a communist, he'd be
alive today. He would probably be to North America what
Neruda is to South. His birthplace says goodbye; leaves
us; is yet to be. Whooping-cranes are already extinct in our
precoital play. It's Madame Ky's menstrual-period. Her
whole country bleeds for the rich bitches of Liberty. And
blood from all Asia soaks down through the earth, drips
out here to starve. India and China, please help, there is a
famine here, an America-famine, there's no longer enough
America to feed Whitman or Poe, and I'm getting very thin.
Oh dropping bombs upon what no longer exists! Glances
traveling through life and death, meeting only at the moment
of and the moment of. Touching. Hart, heart of America, are
we falling through you only to enter an extinct land-guage?
No, we'll breed no more sun. Don't walk in conception.

I don't know the warlords of Chicago (except Henry Rago)
    But I've seen the small squashed octupuses on the
        sidewalks
    The Gold Coast faucets that drip eyes and can't be
        turned off
    And where Cheddi Jagan sweated out all his former
        existences into the elevator-shafts of the blind

I don't know but I can't see much difference between John
    Ashbery or Donald Hall or Barbara Guest or David
    Wagoner or William Meredith or Anne Sexton or
    Sandra Hochman or Thomas Clark or Kenneth Koch
    or others writing
a poem . . . and a U.S. aviator dropping a bomb on Viet-
    namese women
and children: both acts in these hands are in defense of op-
    pression and capitalism

I don't know that fine-print on the sky—the bombers leaving
    They dropped signatures, yours, mine
    After the raid it is so quiet you can hear the crying,
        piping of the unborn babies inside their mothers
    A few fields, where now only wounds take root

I don't know that sea holding its breath in the jungle
    The Viet Cong
  Army whose only camouflage is the people
    They nurse it with fragrant teas
      Compresses of the heart
  It is invisible and laughs in their tatters
   It is a shout
     wreathing up their raised arms
I don't know
  The gasp keeps on falling inside the bucket
              it never hits bottom.

WIDOW'S WINTER

Outside,
the snow is falling into its past . . .
I do want this night to end.
In the fireplace,
a section of ash caves in.

The fall day you were buried
birds went over,
south,
thick enough to carry someone.
They took my gapes of breath
—their fuel?
We are together in some birds, who fail.

I didn't even want to look at your grave,
its heroic little mound
like the peck of dirt we hope to eat in our life . . .

POEM

A man's mortals break over him and
ebb away . . . love, youth, Naomi.
In femoral jungles, light and shadow
play chess; man is present, judging.
Though foundering, I exhale the fate
of unknown cities and races; in my glance,
poison for future gods. The vines
already are clinging to men: they know who to back.
I live, I burn. My mortals,
my guts, break over me and ebb
away . . . love, youth, Naomi.

(FALL) (AND WINTER) (VIETNAM)
(CHICAGO) (1965)

"God created man in His own image"
—Genesis
"Chicago is the architectural showplace of the nation"
—Chicago newspapers

I

A shudder falls from the trees, at night;
the breeze is so light that only the grass on top of graves stirs;
everyone's nose is black with fear;
generals open the burning bodies of children
like letters from home with lace on the edges . . .

2

Oh it's easy to find
Vietnam in Chicago . . . in these bright streets where our
        tears lie
rotting, we are what's lost (knock at your shadow
to ask the way home from death).

3

Men destroy us in their own image,
in their own—lost—likeness. And this year,
even the snowflakes—my last hope—
are twisted into awry hurt shapes,
designs of screams. . . . Napalm: your own afterbirth on fire
        descending . . .

4

Suffering is the same both places. But
at least in Vietnam death is death . . . Here, in this
stainless steel cement tower white concrete glass city,
death is the sole vegetation: death is life, a green magnet.

THE WASP POETS OF AMERICA

for Richard Deutch

The poets' cry—
             Retirement!
To be
      a good gray. The shriek-plumaged
Muse of America slices down
and garlands those who resemble vaults.
Pound is retired,
                bending over his cane as over
a bombsight—
              O Spain, Ethiopia, Vietnam,
your good gray ash poets!
Me and James Dickey
are battling it out for
                  the title
of "The Good Gray Flannel Poet"
Let's suck up to those
                  we would replace,

the fathers
        who sold to us,
                as a whore,
our mother.
Retirement!   Is this
the best
of all possible words? Who
is not a square
        once in
a coffin (which is to say an
America).
      Good blond poets
              —you senile in the womb—
the world is growing young,
           against us.
And we don't even have a pension plan written,
not to mention
poems.

(END) OF SUMMER (1966)

I'm tired of murdering children.
Once, long ago today, they wanted to live;
now I feel Vietnam the place
where rigor mortis is beginning to set-in upon me.

I force silence down the throats of mutes,
down the throats of mating-cries of animals who know they
    are extinct.
The chameleon's death-soliloquy is your voice's pulse;
your scorched forehead a constellation's suicide-note.

A phonograph needle plunges through long black hair,
and stone drips slowly into our veins.
The earth has been squandered by the meek.
And upsidedown in the earth a dead man walks upon my
    soles when I walk.

A baby is crying.
In the swaddling-pages
a baby.

"Don't cry. No Solomon's-sword can
divide you from the sky.
You are one. Fly."

I'm tired, so tired.
I have sleep to do.
I have work to dream.

William Kilborn Knott was born in Carson City, MI on February 17, 1940 and died while undergoing heart surgery in Bay City, MI on March 12, 2014. He taught poetry at Emerson College in Boston, MA for nearly 27 years, retiring in 2008. In his lifetime he published 13 books with traditional publishing houses, and was awarded the Iowa Poetry Prize and a Guggenheim fellowship. In his final two decades he self-published innumerable small pamphlets and larger collections to be freely given away. These books commonly comprised thematic groupings from his large and ever-growing body of work—titles such as *Sixty Poems of Love and Homage* (1994) and *Collected Comic Poems 1960-2000* (2000)—along with periodic sets of new work. The last of these self-published volumes was the atypically huge *Collected Poetry* (488 pp., often with multiple poems per page) uploaded to Amazon two weeks before his death. A posthumous collection, *I am Flying into Myself: Selected Poems, 1960-2014*, edited by Thomas Lux, appeared in 2017.

*

Richard Hell is the author of several books of fiction, poetry, essays, notebooks, autobiography, and collaborations including *The Voidoid, Go Now, Godlike, Across the Years, Artifact, Hot and Cold, I Dreamed I Was a Very Clean Tramp, Massive Pissed Love, Wanna Go Out?* by Theresa Stern (with Tom Verlaine) and *Psychopts* (with Christopher Wool). He has also been a musician and his most recent album/CD/stream is *Destiny Street Complete* (2021). He lives in New York.